CHARLES DICKENS

CHARLES DICKENS

Christopher Martin

The Rourke Corporation, Inc.
Vero Beach, FL 32964

Life and Works

The Brontës
Joseph Conrad
Charles Dickens
T. S. Eliot
Ernest Hemingway
D.H. Lawrence
Katherine Mansfield
George Orwell
Shakespeare
John Steinbeck
H.G. Wells
Virginia Woolf

Cover illustration by David Armitage

Text © 1990 The Rourke Corporation, Inc.

Library of Congress Cataloging-in-Publication Data
Martin, Christopher, *1939–*
     Charles Dickens/by Christopher Martin.
         p. cm. – (Life and works)
     Includes bibliographical references.
     Summary: Explores the life and work of the nineteenth-
century English novelist.
     ISBN 0–86593–016–3
     1. Dickens, Charles, 1812–1870 – Juvenile literature.
2. Novelists, English – 19th century – Biography – Juvenile
literature. [1. Dickens, Charles, 1812–1870. 2. Authors,
English.] I. Title. II. Series.
PR4581.M38   1990
821'.8 – dc20
[B]
[92]   89–28320
                                                              CIP
                                                               AC

Contents

1
Singular Abilities

There are strange contradictions in the work and character of Charles Dickens. The American critic Edmund Wilson described him in the terms of his own creation, as the "two Scrooges." He was the creator of gentle, innocent Little Nell, yet he also wrote terrifying, brutal murder scenes. He was the relentless critic of a Victorian society obsessed with wealth, yet he finally exhausted himself in an obsessive pursuit of money. A genial extrovert, he invented Mr. Pickwick and the Victorian Christmas ideal, yet he hid within his personality, as the writer Thomas Carlyle noted, "dark fateful silent elements, tragical to look upon, and, hiding amid dazzling radiances as of the sun, the elements of death itself."

In later life Dickens liked to claim impressive Staffordshire ancestors. In fact his paternal grandparents were servants: butler and housekeeper to John Crewe M.P. at Crewe Hall, in Cheshire. Crewe helped his housekeeper, after her husband died, to place her sons in the world. John, Charles's father, became a clerk in the Naval Pay Office in London. The salary was good enough for him to marry Elizabeth Barrow, daughter of a fellow official. They settled first near the naval base in Portsmouth. Their home, at Mile End Terrace, Portsea, was the birthplace of Charles John Huffam Dickens, the second of their eight children, on February 7, 1812.

John Dickens had great charm and ability, yet he was never able to live within his means. Charles's later boyhood was shadowed by the chronic debt problems of

Opposite *Charles Dickens at the height of his fame and power as a writer. This photograph was taken in 1861, when* Great Expectations *appeared in book form.*

8

his feckless father. For a time, all went well. In 1817, John was given a new post in Chatham dockyard in Kent; here the Royal Navy built and repaired its ships. The next few years were the golden time of Charles's childhood. The house in Ordnance Terrace stood on a hill overlooking the Medway River. Nearby was Rochester, with its ancient castle ruin and cathedral: "Fine place – glorious pile – frowning walls – tottering arches – dark nooks – crumbling staircases," as Mr. Jingle of *The Pickwick Papers* later defined it. Dickens, loved the city, which appears in his first and last novels. He looked back on the twin towns and their river and countryside with deepest affection.

John Dickens could be a wonderful father. Charles went with him to explore the dockyard and the fascinating marine stores. He and his father took long walks through Cobham Park and the marshes near Cooling, where they saw the children's graves later used in *Great Expectations*. On Gad's Hill they admired the fine house that Dickens later bought, remembering his father's promise that "If you were to work hard, you might some day come to live in it."

Dickens's first schooling came from his mother and from a local dame school. His young nurse stimulated his vivid imagination with her horrific bedtime stories that left him "rigid with terror." He was always fascinated by the supernatural, and the stories taught him about "the dark corners" of his mind. There was the Chatham shipwright Chips, haunted by a devil in the shape of a rat. There was Captain Murderer, who killed, ate and "picked the bones of several wives." On his wedding morning, the Captain always caused both sides of the way to the church to be planted with curious flowers, and when his bride said:

> "Dear Captain Murderer, I never saw flowers like these before; what are they called?" He answered, "They are called Garnish for house-lamb," and laughed at his ferocious practical joke in a horrid manner . . . with a very sharp show of teeth, then displayed for the first time. . .
>
> (*Nurse's Stories*: "The Uncommercial Traveller")

Dickens also became a "terrible boy to read," devouring the small library of reprinted classics that his father

Opposite *John Dickens, Charles's father, was a clerk in the Royal Navy Pay Office. Never able to live within his means, he became the model for the debtor figures, Mr. Micawber and William Dorrit, in his son's novels.*

had collected: picaresque romances such as *Don Quixote* and *Gil Blas,* and eighteenth-century novels including *Roderick Random, Tom Jones* and a particular favorite, *The Vicar of Wakefield*. This "glorious host," and *The Arabian Nights,* he read "with greedy relish," acting out the adventures in his mind.

A scene from Henry Fielding's Tom Jones *(1749), one of the eighteenth-century novels that Dickens read avidly as a boy. He used Fielding's picaresque adventure form in his own work.*

At Chatham also, Dickens discovered his life-long delight in the theater. He went to the pantomime in London and saw the famous clown Grimaldi. At the tiny Theatre Royal in Rochester he delighted in the "glories" of live theater: melodrama, farce, tragedy, no matter how badly performed. The witches in *Macbeth* made his heart "leap with terror."

The family sometimes went to a Baptist Chapel in Chatham. The minister had a son, William Giles, an Oxford graduate who kept a small school. When Charles joined his class, Giles soon recognized his outstanding abilities, and the boy began to flourish. William's sister left the first word-picture of Dickens: "a very handsome boy with long curly hair of a light colour." He was "capital company" and "took great delight in Fifth of November festivities round the bonfire."

Then in 1822, when he was ten, Dickens's life changed dramatically for the worse. John Dickens was transferred to London. Charles worked out his term with William Giles, who gave him an influential leaving present, *The Bee*, a literary miscellany (a form later much used by Dickens) by his favorite writer, Oliver Goldsmith.

Then he traveled alone to London by stagecoach. "Have I ever lost the smell of damp straw in which I was packed – like game – and forwarded carriage paid, to the Cross Keys, Wood Street, Cheapside, London – I consumed my sandwiches in solitude and dreariness, and it rained hard all the way, and I thought life sloppier than I had expected it to be," he recalled in his essay "Dullborough Town."

The Dickens family had settled in a cramped house in Camden Town, a new settlement near London. There was open countryside nearby, but this was already threatened by the mushrooming growth of the city and was very different from the golden fields of Rochester. Yet he now discovered a new passion: the streets of London, whose life and contrasts he never tired of observing:

Streams of people apparently without end poured on and on, jostling each other in the crowd and hurrying forward, while vehicles of all shapes and makes, mingled up together in one moving mass like running water, lent their ceaseless roar to swell the noise and tumult . . .

The rags of the squalid ballad singer fluttered in the rich
light that showed the goldsmith's treasures, pale and
pinched-up faces hovered about the windows where
there was tempting food, hungry eyes wandered over
the profusion . . .

(*Nicholas Nickleby*, Chapter 22)

In Sketches by Boz, *Dickens recorded his sharply observed impressions of life in London's streets. This Cruikshank drawing illustrates the essay "The Streets: Morning."*

13

Dickens's older sister won a scholarship to the Royal Academy of Music, but he was not placed in any school. His father was busy with a "deed," drawn up to satisfy his creditors. "So I degenerated into cleaning his boots of a morning . . . and going on such poor errands as arose out of our poor way of living," he recalled bitterly.

Then something turned up. The Dickens's lodger, James Lamert, had become manager of a shoe-blacking business carried on at Hungerford Stairs, where Charing Cross Station now stands. He suggested that Charles should work there. If his parents were pleased to have one child provided for, Charles was not; he was sick with despair at being ". . . so easily cast away." He began his work in the rat-infested warehouse, covering and labeling pots of blacking. His workmates were laboring boys in ragged aprons and paper caps:

> No words can express the secret agony of my soul, as I sunk into this companionship; compared these everyday associates with those of my happier childhood; and felt my early hopes of growing up to be a learned and distinguished man, crushed in my bosom.

(Autobiographical Fragment: Forster's *Life of Dickens*)

At home, conditions deteriorated. Tradesmen shouted up at the windows, demanding payment. The vague Mrs. Dickens, later portrayed by her son as Mrs. Micawber and Mrs. Nickleby, now planned to open a school, moving the family to a large house in Gower Street for the purpose. A brass plate, inscribed "Mrs. Dickens' Establishment" was the only practical part of the plan. "Nobody ever came to the school, nor do I recollect that anybody ever proposed to come," noted her son. Their possessions went steadily to the pawnshop. Charles even had to take the much-loved books to a drunken bookseller.

Finally, John Dickens was arrested and sent to the Marshalsea debtors' prison. He declared to his broken-hearted son that the sun had set on him forever. He fearfully warned Charles "to take warning by the Marshalsea, and to observe that if a man had twenty pounds a year, and spent nineteen pounds nineteen shillings and sixpence he would be happy; but that a shilling spent the other way would make him wretched."

Opposite *Elizabeth Dickens, Charles's vague, impractical mother, became the model for his fictitious creations, Mrs. Nickleby and Mrs. Micawber.*

The home collapsed and the family joined the father in prison. Charles was boarded outside, though he visited every day, observing prison life so closely that it was ". . . written indelibly on my memory." He became a lonely drifter, debating whether to spend his pennies on stale pastries or a slice of pudding. "When I had no money, I took a turn in Covent Garden and stared at the pineapples." He gave himself treats, entering a public house and ordering "your very best – the VERY best – ale . . . They served me the ale . . . and the landlord's wife, opening the little half-door and bending down gave me a kiss that was half admiring and half compassionate, but all womanly and good, I am sure."

When his mother died, leaving him some money, John Dickens was able to escape the Marshalsea and take his family back to Camden Town. Charles now worked near Covent Garden, toiling at his blacking pots in the window of the new premises. Shamed at this public display of his son, his father determined he should return to school – although Dickens noted angrily that his mother was "warm" for him to continue at Warren's Blacking. For years afterward he avoided the scenes of his boyhood humiliation, which ". . . made me cry, after my eldest child could speak . . . I often forget in my dreams even that I am a man and wander desolately back to that time of my life."

In 1824 Dickens joined Wellington Academy, a private school in North London. The Headmaster (later portrayed as Mr. Creakle in *David Copperfield*) was "by far the most ignorant man I have ever had the pleasure to know," eager only to hit boys with his "bloated mahogany ruler." But Dickens was determined to do well, and made rapid progress. He was remembered by friends as "a short, stout, jolly-looking youth, full of fun," but particularly neat in his dress, a reaction to his former shabbiness. Like other boys, he trained white mice, produced plays in a toy theater and read the *Terrific Register,* in which "there was always a pool of blood and at least one body."

Three years later, his mother found him a place as clerk in a firm of solicitors. Here he acquired a lasting antipathy for the law, which he saw as dedicated only "to make money for itself." His acute observation later allowed him to re-create portraits of lawyers with "their

Opposite *When David Copperfield visits a public house to celebrate his birthday, Dickens was recalling an actual incident from his own lonely London boyhood, after his father was imprisoned for debt.*

17

air of knowing something to everybody's disadvantage," and of shabby, stuffy law offices.

With a salary, he could now enjoy London life. He liked the cheap theaters, such as Astley's with its circus shows, and the so-called private theaters where members of the public could pay to act on stage. He went to see Charles Mathews who performed comic plays in which he took all the parts. Mathews's style left its mark on the comic dialogue in Dickens's novels. Dickens still loved to explore London's maze of streets. "I thought I knew something of the town," said a fellow clerk, "but he knew it all from Bow to Brentford." He observed the people, too, and could imitate the varied street language of the "low population" of the city.

When John Dickens was retired from the Navy Pay Office, he turned to journalism as a new career, learning shorthand to become a parliamentary reporter. Charles, too, saw this as an escape from the law, "a very little world, and a very dull one." With the iron determination that became typical of him, he too mastered the complexities of shorthand, learning ". . . the changes that were wrung upon dots . . . the wonderful vagaries that were played by circles; the unaccountable consequences that resulted from marks like flies' legs."

Still only sixteen, he now left his clerk's post to become a reporter in Doctors' Commons, a muddle of ancient courts in a "lazy old nook" near St. Paul's Cathedral. The Commons confirmed Dickens's sour view of the law: it was full of "worm-eaten old books . . . and self-important looking personages full of conceit and silliness." The robed judges reminded him of bad actors. However, the job gave him more liberty, and he read avidly in the British Museum to continue his self-education.

Meanwhile, he had fallen in love with Maria Beadnell, a banker's daughter. She had dark ringlets, bright eyes and, like Dora Spenlow in *David Copperfield*, a "prettily pettish manner":

> I was a captive and a slave . . . she was more than human to me. She was a Fairy, a Sylph, I don't know what she was . . . everything that everybody ever wanted. I was swallowed up in an abyss of love in an instant.

(*David Copperfield*, Chapter 26)

Opposite *"No words can express the agony of my soul": a striking illustration from Forster's* Life of Dickens, *showing Charles as an eleven-year-old, working at Warren's Blacking Factory at Hungerford Stairs near Charing Cross in 1823.*

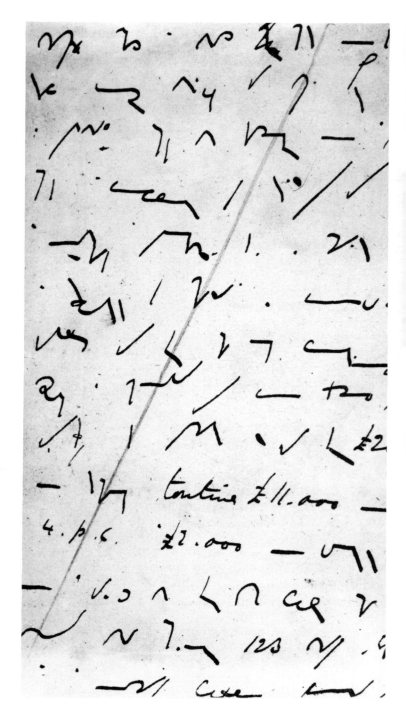

A page of Dickens's shorthand notes. Learning this skill changed him from lawyer's clerk to journalist, and was therefore the basis of his writing career.

His love was unrequited, though she enjoyed torment-
ing him. Her parents thought "Mr. Dickin" totally
unsuitable. Anxious to improve his financial status, he
now thought of the stage as a career. A cold prevented
him attending a vital audition, however. Another chance
then appeared. An uncle, John Barrow, had started a
new paper reporting Parliamentary affairs. He already
employed John Dickens. In 1832, Charles also joined the
Mirror of Parliament. He soon made "a great splash," as
being in "the very highest rank, not merely for accuracy
in reporting but for marvellous quickness in transcript."

Despite his new success, he fared no better with Maria and became deeply unhappy. In despair, he wrote her a last letter in May 1832: "I have never loved and I can never love any creature breathing but yourself." She ignored him, and he went his way.

In December 1833, Dickens's career entered a new phase. He had begun to write little fictional sketches of London life and people. One story he "dropped stealthily one evening at twilight, with fear and trembling, into a dark letterbox, in a dark office, up a dark court in Fleet Street." The office belonged to the *Monthly Magazine.* When the new edition appeared, Dickens bought a copy and saw his article ". . . in all the glory of print: on which occasion I walked down to Westminster Hall, and turned into it for half-an-hour, because my eyes were so dimmed with joy and pride."

2
Rising
Like a Rocket

As he scribbled shorthand in the House of Commons gallery, Dickens watched some momentous legislation: the Reform Bill of 1832, which abolished an outdated and unfair voting system; the first real Factory Act, which banned the employment of children under nine in factory work; the abolition of slavery; the New Poor Law. Yet he was not impressed by Parliament, dominated as it was by the interests of wealthy landowners.

Night after night, I record predictions that never come to pass, professions that are never fulfilled, explanations that are only meant to mystify. I wallow in words. Britannia, that unfortunate female, is always before me, like a trussed fowl: skewered through and through with office pens, and bound hand and foot with red tape.

(*David Copperfield*, Chapter 43)

Opposite *As a reporter, Dickens traveled the country to watch England's primitive pre-Victorian democracy in action. He later recorded some of his impressions in the comic confusion of the Eatanswill by-election in* The Pickwick Papers.

In 1833, his talents won Dickens a post as Parliamentary reporter with a Liberal daily newspaper, the *Morning Chronicle*. He now began to travel to political meetings all over the country, sometimes enjoying races with the *Times* man to get news back to London.

Meanwhile he continued his sketches of London. He signed them "Boz," a pen-name derived from the family pet-name for Charles's youngest brother, Augustus. He was earning a good salary and could afford to dress as a dandy, with fancy waistcoats or "very handsome blue cloak with velvet facings."

25

Greenwich Fair.

Among his growing acquaintance was a publisher, John Macrone. He considered the sketches "capital value" and suggested making them into a book. In February 1836, *Sketches by Boz* was published. Reviewers saw Dickens as "a man of unquestionable talent and of great and correct observation." He was "a close observer of human nature" with the power "of producing tears as well as laughter." The collection is two-sided in its study of William IV's London. There is charm and comedy in "London Recreations" or "Greenwich Fair," but, in a darker vein, Dickens shows us London slums in St. Giles:

> . . . wretched houses with broken windows patched with rags and paper; every room let to a different family – filth everywhere – clothes drying and slops emptying from the windows: girls of fourteen or fifteen, with matted hair, walking about barefoot, and in white great-coats, almost their only covering . . .

("Ginshops," *Sketches by Boz*)

He watches a lonely woman beggar, singing to earn some money:

> A brutal laugh at her weak voice is all she has gained. The tears fall thick and fast down her own pale face; the child is cold and hungry, and its low half-stifled wailing adds to the misery of its wretched mother, as she moans aloud, and sinks despairingly down, on a cold damp doorstep. Singing . . . bitter mockery! . . . The weak tremulous voice tells a fearful tale of want and famishing.

("The Streets: Night," *Sketches by Boz*)

"Newgate" is the finest piece, reflecting Dickens's lasting interest in prisons. Here Dickens moves from the brilliant reporting of the actual – the "terrible little faces" of the boy pickpockets; the double grating that divided prisoner from visitor – into fiction, in his picture of the condemned man who dreams of escape as he waits for execution at dawn. He wakes and "He is the condemned felon again, guilty and despairing; and in two hours more will be dead."

The best review of *Sketches* came from George Hogarth, a fellow journalist on the *Chronicle*. Dickens had known

Opposite Sketches by Boz *describes London's fun and vitality in the time of William IV. This Cruikshank drawing shows the public dancing arena at Greenwich Fair.*

George Cruikshank

him since 1834 and had visited his home where he met his daughters, Catherine, Mary and Georgina. The women were to play a large part in his life. He was attracted to "placid, kindly Kate" and she found him "very gentlemanly and pleasant." The whole family was pleased when Dickens asked Catherine to marry him in 1835.

It was not an easy engagement. Dickens was ferociously busy, sitting "chained to his table" in his rooms at Furnival's Inn. When Catherine expressed impatience, he wrote her some stern letters reprimanding her. After his sufferings with Maria, he was determined to be master of this relationship.

Dickens now received an offer from the publishers Chapman & Hall to write a twenty-episode serial about "manners and life in the country." It would appear in monthly parts, a new form of publication. The artist, Robert Seymour, would provide comic drawings about a sporting club; Dickens would write the text. He had no interest in country sports, however, and suggested using "a freer range of English scenes and people." The publishers agreed. Then, noted Dickens with dramatic simplicity, "I thought of Mr. Pickwick."

The serial was slow to take off and was threatened with disaster when Seymour, angry and distressed at the change in his first plan, suddenly shot himself. But when a new artist, Hablot K. Browne, who called himself "Phiz" (and who was to be the outstanding Dickens illustrator) was found and the cockney Sam Weller entered the story, *Pickwick* began its astonishing course of success. Its sales reached 40,000 a month, and critics now found it "irresistibly good . . . uproarious in its fun." Everyone enjoyed it.

As for its author, reviewers noted that " 'Boz' marches on triumphantly, and has taken possession of the ear and the hearts, too, of his countrymen." "Boz-mania" swept London; there were Pickwick hats and songs, Weller boots and joke books. "PICKWICK TRIUMPHANT," noted Dickens in a letter. When he appeared at a London theater, ". . . with long brown hair falling in silky masses over his temples, dressed in the very height of the existing fashion," the audience gave him a standing ovation. In November he wrote to his publishers: "If I were to live a hundred years, and

Opposite The Sketches *also have a darker side, observing the ugliness and overcrowding of notorious slum areas. This is a street of secondhand clothes shops in London's St. Giles.*

write three novels in each, I should never be so proud of any of them as I am of Pickwick."

Pickwick has a charm that defies criticism. G.K. Chesterton, the Edwardian writer, considered that "it emits that sense of everlasting youth – a sense as of the gods gone wandering in England."

page 2

Yet some critics have seen *Pickwick* as so fragmentary that it scarcely makes up a novel. Dickens saw this, but knew that he was using a form, the picaresque adventure, that had important forbears, *Don Quixote* and *Tom Jones* among them. He enjoyed the sketch form that the part-work gave; he could introduce sudden contrasts (like the interpolated short stories), respond to current interests, and develop a character that readers liked.

Moreover, the book is not entirely haphazard. Dickens created continuity by means of recurring characters, a continuous story-line and places revisited. He gave the collection a sense of progress in the aging of the constant characters and in the deepening knowledge they acquire of each other, the world and themselves. Pickwick is, like the over-imaginative Don Quixote, instructed in the realities of the world by his equivalent of Sancho Panza, Sam Weller. He experiences a "fall" from the bright paradise of the early chapters to the horrors of the Fleet prison, where he is sent after refusing to pay for his breach of promise to Mrs. Bardell:

> The place was intolerably dirty and the smell of tobacco smoke suffocating. There was a perpetual slamming and banging of doors as the people went in and out; and the noise of their voices and footsteps echoed and re-echoed through the passages constantly. A young woman, with a child in her arms, who seemed scarcely able to crawl, from emaciation and misery, was walking up and down the passage in conversation with her husband, who had no other place to see her in. As they passed Mr. Pickwick, he could hear the female sob . . .

(*The Pickwick Papers*, Chapter 41)

Dickens married Catherine Hogarth on April 2, 1836, and went on a brief honeymoon at Chalk in the Kent countryside near Chatham. Then they settled happily in the rooms at Furnival's Inn. When they had left there later, Dickens looked back on this first home with affection: he would never be ". . . so happy again as in these chambers three storeys high . . . never so happy again – never if I roll in wealth and fame." Sixteen-year-old Mary Hogarth came to live with them to be her sister Catherine's companion. "Winning, happy and amiable," she worshiped her brother-in-law.

Opposite *Mr. Pickwick was the first of Dickens's great comic characters. This illustration of the first meeting of the Pickwick Club was done by Robert Seymour, who shot himself shortly after the serial began.*

Dickens was working at too many projects: a play, a novel called *Gabriel Vardon* (later renamed *Barnaby Rudge*), reporting for the *Chronicle,* as well as writing *Pickwick's* monthly parts. In autumn 1836, he finally gave up reporting, when he was invited to edit a magazine, *Bentley's Miscellany.* At Christmas he met John Forster, who became his "dear and trusty friend," acting as his unofficial adviser and agent in his sometimes quarrelsome dealings with publishers. Forster's practical skill in wordly affairs made a perfect complement to Dickens's writing talent.

The birth of a son, the first of his ten children, forced Dickens to find a larger house at 48 Doughty Street, then an exclusive thoroughfare with gates at each end and a porter in a gold-laced hat. For a time, family happiness continued. He was now writing *Oliver Twist* as a serial for *Bentley's.* He sometimes liked to write in the drawing room among his visitors, as his brother-in-law recalled:

> "What you here!" he exclaimed. "I'll bring down my work." It was his monthly portion of "Oliver Twist". . . In a few minutes he returned, manuscript in hand, and while he was pleasantly discoursing, he recommenced his writing . . . it was interesting to watch . . . the mind and muscle working . . . as new thoughts were being dropped upon the paper. And to note the working brow, the set of the mouth, with the tongue tightly pressed against the closed lips, as was his habit.

Then came a shattering blow. One night in May 1837, after a visit to the theater, Mary Hogarth, still only seventeen, who seemed "in perfect health and her usual delightful spirits," died suddenly, apparently of a heart attack. Dickens, who had held her as she died, was stunned with grief. "I have lost the dearest friend I ever had," he wrote in a letter. "Words cannot describe the pride I felt in her, and the devoted attachment I bore her . . . I solemnly believe that so perfect a creature never breathed. I knew her inmost heart."

He wore her ring all his life; he kept her clothes until they rotted. He wanted to be buried beside her. Mary haunted his dreams and appeared repeatedly as the virginal young heroine in his novels: Little Nell, Florence Dombey, Little Dorrit.

Opposite *Mr. Pickwick skating at Dingley Dell. This is one of many Dickensian celebrations of Christmas. The artist, Hablot Browne ("Phiz"), became the classic illustrator of Dickens's works.*

Dickens gradually regained his energy. Some doubted if he could maintain his pace. The *Quarterly Review* warned that "Mr. Dickens writes too often and too fast . . . he has risen like a rocket, and he will come down like the stick." *Oliver Twist* soon pushed aside such criticism.

Dickens's first intention was to attack the working of the 1834 New Poor Law that created the grim Union Workhouse system as a remedy for poverty. He had watched the Act passed by Parliament, and, to the end of his life, thought the "great blank barren Union House" was worse than prison in its effects on the poor and weak. Above all, he hated the meager diet, which was aimed to make paupers avoid the workhouses but ignored the needs of children. He shows his anger in the most famous passage he ever wrote, where Oliver Twist asks for more:

Opposite Catherine Hogarth, daughter of a leading journalist, became Dickens's wife in 1836. This portrait is by Dickens's artist friend, Daniel Maclise.

Another Maclise sketch, showing Dickens, Catherine (center) and her younger sister Mary, who shared the Dickens home in Doughty Street. Mary died suddenly in 1837, when she was only seventeen, leaving Dickens heartbroken.

Above *Oliver Twist asks for more. Dickens symbolizes the cruelty, meanness and corruption of the workings of the 1834 New Poor Law; from the 1947 movie of Oliver Twist.*
Opposite *The master criminal Fagin in the condemned cell at Newgate at the end of Oliver Twist.*

Child as he was, he was desperate with hunger, and reckless with misery. He rose from the table, and advancing to the master, basin and spoon in hand, said, somewhat alarmed at his own temerity, "Please, sir, I want some more."

The Master was a fat, healthy man; but he turned very pale. He gazed in stupefied astonishment on the small rebel for some seconds, and then clung for support to the copper. The assistants were paralysed with wonder; the boys with fear.

"What!" said the Master at length, in a faint voice.

"Please, sir," replied Oliver, "I want some more."

(*Oliver Twist*, Chapter 2)

Oliver is a lonely, outcast child, of a type that Dickens was to explore later in great depth. If he is an uninteresting figure in himself, scenes in which he is involved have a terrifying, dream-like intensity, as when he is recaptured by Nancy after his stay at Mr. Brownlow's, or when Fagin and Monks watch him sleeping at Mrs. Mylie's cottage.

"Newgate" novels, based on real criminal cases, were popular in the 1830s. Some thought them dangerous because they showed criminals sympathetically, explaining their crime by poverty. Dickens denied that *Oliver Twist* belonged to this genre; he shows the sordid ugliness of the criminal's life. Yet he is deeply fascinated by his evil creations. The monstrous Fagin is at the center of a criminal network that exploits boys who are drawn to crime by ignorance or need:

> As he glided stealthily along, creeping beneath the shelter of the walls and doorways, the hideous old man seemed like some loathsome reptile, engendered by the slime and darkness through which he moved; crawling forth by night, in search of some rich offal for a meal.

(Oliver Twist, Chapter 19)

The Artful Dodger is a colorful leader among the boy criminals, displaying charm and cheek even at his trial. Bill Sikes is a desperate and clever criminal. Fear, as well as fury, lead him to murder the loyal Nancy, in one of the most powerful scenes in a Dickens novel:

> The sun – the bright sun, that brings back, not light alone, but new life, and hope, and freshness to man . . . it lighted up the room where the murdered woman lay. It did. He tried to shut it out but it would stream in. If the sight had been a ghastly one in the dull morning, what was it, now, in all that brilliant light! . . . And there was the body – mere flesh and blood, no more – but such flesh, and so much blood!

(Oliver Twist, Chapter 48)

A desperate attempt to escape capture ends in Sikes's horrific death by hanging, as he plunges from a rooftop, entangled in his own rope.

Opposite *Oliver learns a new trade: he watches the Artful Dodger pick Mr.Brownlow's pocket. Oliver is the first of Dickens's lonely, outcast children, a type created from his own harsh experiences as a boy.*

3 The Inimitable

Even before *Oliver Twist* was finished, Dickens had begun *Nicholas Nickleby*. Its starting point was the contemporary scandal of the "Yorkshire schools," which, advertising with the sinister promise of "no vacations," took unwanted children away from their families on a permanent basis, in return for payment. They were notorious for cruelty. Dickens saw them as part of the "monstrous neglect of education in England . . . These Yorkshire schools were the lowest and most rotten round in the whole ladder."

In January 1838, Dickens and the artist Phiz went to Yorkshire in search of material, pretending to be interested in placing a child at such a school. At so-called Bowes Academy, near Greta Bridge, they met the one-eyed William Shaw. Ten children had become blind in his charge and there were twenty-five boys' graves in the nearby churchyard. Dickens's sharp eye recorded what he needed for his serial:

The pupils'. . . pale and haggard faces, lank and bony figures, children with the countenances of old men, deformities with irons upon their limbs . . . every ugliness or distortion that told of unnatural aversion conceived by parents for their offspring or of young lives which had been one horrible endurance of cruelty and neglect.

(*Nicholas Nickleby*, Chapter 8)

Opposite *"The internal economy of Dotheboys' Hall": Mrs. Squeers doses the pupils with "medicine" that will kill their appetites. Nicholas Nickleby and Mr. Squeers watch the school's methods; in the foreground, Wackford Squeers tries on new boots stolen from another boy. In 1838, Dickens and Phiz went north to see such "Yorkshire schools."*

Mr. Squeers in the novel is the "block-headed impostor," whose education "system" Dickens lashes with sarcasm:

> "We go upon the practical mode of teaching, Nickleby; the regular education system. C–l–e–a–n, clean, verb active, to make bright, to scour. W–i–n, win, d–e–r, der, winder, a casement. When the boy knows this out of the book, he goes and does it!"

(*Nicholas Nickleby*, Chapter 8)

Dotheboys' Hall is only the beginning of Nicholas's adventures. There are swift changes of mood, from satire, to sentiment, to melodrama. A slender thread of plot and a lightly handled love theme string together the comic set-pieces, which are full of joyful energy. Those involving Vincent Crummles and his strolling players are particularly fresh and lively. Dickens was at his closest to the theater in this book: the critic John Ruskin said that his novels were "created in a circle of stage fire."

Dickens was now at the height of his youthful powers. His portrait by his friend Daniel Maclise was shown at the Royal Academy. He entered high society. In London's great houses, he met and mixed with the outstanding people of his time. "What a face is his to meet in a drawing room," said the poet Leigh Hunt. "It has the life and soul in it of fifty human beings." He was elected to the exclusive Athenaeum Club, reserved for those "known for their scientific or literary attainments."

With his growing family, he needed a bigger home. Devonshire Terrace, an imposing Georgian house near Regent's Park, reflected his new status. Dickens now worked in a well-stocked library, overlooking the large garden where his children played. He had become the gentleman that his father, still hopelessly in debt, had aspired to be.

His next literary project was, at first, a failure. *Master Humphrey's Clock* was a collection of tales told by a club of friends. A slump in sales forced Dickens to bring forward another idea for a "little child story" that he expanded into *The Old Curiosity Shop*. It began as part of the *Clock* but, because of "the intense interest excited by the natural and sweetly pathetic story," it took over the whole magazine.

Opposite Master Humphrey's Clock, *edited by Dickens (seen standing by the clock doors) was the second of several magazine projects that he experimented with in his writing career. The* Clock *was a failure, until* The Old Curiosity Shop *took it over and it became a triumphant success.*

WOODCUT ILLUSTRATION,

By "Phiz."

As in the Original Prospectus to

"MASTER HUMPHREY'S CLOCK."

The grotesque evil dwarf, Quilp, who pursues Little Nell and her grandfather during their restless journey across England.

In his own time, Little Nell was one of Dickens's most admired creations. Modern readers find her sentimental, yet her fear and bewilderment as she and her grandfather wander across England to escape from the hideous evil dwarf, Quilp, are part of an impressive picture of a child's vision of the world:

> Evening came on. They were still wandering up and down, with fewer people about them, but with the same sense of solitude in their own breasts, and the same indifference from all around . . . Why had they ever come to this noisy town? . . . They were but an atom, here, in a mountain heap of misery.

(*The Old Curiosity Shop*, Chapter 44)

Contrasted with Nell is the grotesque Quilp: ". . . as sharp as a ferret and as cunning as a weasel" who "ate hard eggs, shell and all . . . drank boiling tea without winking, bit his fork and spoon till they bent." He meets an ugly death by drowning in the Thames: "It toyed and sported with its ghastly freight . . . until, tired of the ugly play thing, it flung it on a swamp – a dismal place where pirates had swung in chains . . . and left it there to bleach."

His fate is set against the celebrated climax of the story – the death of Little Nell. Although Dickens was "inundated with imploring letters recommending poor Little Nell to mercy," he decided she should die in a remote Shropshire village, exhausted by her wanderings. Into the death scene, he wove his own painful memories of Mary Hogarth: ". . . old wounds bleed afresh when I only think of the way of doing it. Dear Mary died yesterday when I think of this sad story."

She was dead. No sleep so beautiful and calm, so free from trace of pain, so fair to look upon. She seemed a creature fresh from the hand of God, and waiting for the breath of life: not one who had lived and suffered death. She was dead. Dear, gentle, patient, noble Nell was dead . . .

(*The Old Curiosity Shop*, Chapter 71)

"Patient noble Nell was dead": Victorian readers found the sentimental death of Little Nell deeply affecting.

The Dickens children did not go to the United States with their parents in 1842. Daniel Maclise painted a group portrait of them (with the family's pet raven Grip) for their parents to take on their tour. From the left: Katey, Walter, Charley and Mamie.

The scene showed Dickens's insight into the tastes and feelings of his contemporaries. His readers were moved to tears. The judge Lord Jeffrey was found weeping over Nell in his library; the politician Daniel O'Connell threw his copy out of a train window, shouting, "He should not have killed her!" Crowds on New York pier, watching the arrival of the ship that carried the fatal issue, shouted to the crew, "Is Little Nell dead?"

Dickens now turned back to the much delayed *Barnaby Rudge*. After a slow start, the story came alive in its picture of the violence of the anti-Catholic Gordon riots in London in 1780. "I think I can make a better riot than Lord George Gordon did," he told Forster, and used his intimate knowledge of the city by night to great effect:

If Bedlam gates had been flung open wide, there would not have issued forth such maniacs as the frenzy of that night had made . . . on the skull of one drunken lad . . . the lead from the roof came streaming down in a shower of liquid fire, white hot, melting his head like wax . . . But of all the howling throng not one learned mercy from, nor sickened at, these sights; nor was the fierce, besotted, senseless rage of one man glutted.

(*Barnaby Rudge*, Chapter 55)

After finishing this serial, Dickens proposed to take a rest from writing. A long-considered project to visit the United States now became a reality. His work was popular there and he was attracted by the democratic ideals of the New World. The American writer Washington Irving promised him "a triumph from one end of the States to the other." His wife was to go with him, but the children would stay behind. "I cannot describe to you the glow into which I rise," Dickens told an American journalist, "when I think of the wonders that await us in your mighty land."

The Britannia, *one of the first transatlantic steamships, carried Dickens and his wife to the United States in January 1842.*

In January 1842, they endured an uncomfortable voyage on the paddle steamship *Britannia* before enjoying a wild reception in Boston. People leaped aboard to shake Dickens's hand. He seemed, said a Boston publisher, "on fire with curiosity and alive as I never saw mortal before." As the couple passed from city to city, there were balls, dinners, welcoming ceremonies of all kinds. "There never was a King or Emperor upon the Earth so cheered and followed by crowds," Dickens told Forster. In New York, enthusiasm turned to hysteria, and Dickens became exhausted and angry, as people plucked pinches of fur from his coat as he passed.

The welcoming mood changed when Dickens mentioned international copyright. British writing, including his own, was republished in the United States without payment to the author. He reminded his audiences of the novelist Sir Walter Scott dying in financial difficulty while "not one grateful dollar piece" came to save him. The powerful American press, which did well out of this piracy, turned against Dickens: "We want no advice upon this subject, and it will be better for Mr. Dickens if he refrains from introducing the matter."

When he traveled south, Dickens was disappointed with the rough politics of Washington. He was physically sickened by the almost universal habit of chewing tobacco and spitting; he even noticed a "spit box" beside the President's chair in the White House. He was morally sickened by slavery and its taskmasters "who notch the ears of men and women . . . learn to write with pens of red-hot iron on the human face . . . breaking living limbs as did the soldiery who mocked and slew the saviour of the world."

American Notes was the swiftly written result of his visit. It was received with anger in the United States. Even his American writer friend, Edgar Allan Poe, thought it "one of the most suicidal productions ever." Richard Dana, another author, declared, "His journey to America has been a Moscow expedition for his fame."

There were American notes also in *Martin Chuzzlewit*, his next novel. Transatlantic critics were further annoyed by his comments on "that republic, but yesterday, let loose upon her noble course, and today so maimed and lame, so full of sores and ulcers . . . that her best friends turn from the loathsome creature with disgust."

Opposite *One of the earliest photographs of Dickens: a daguerrotype portrait of 1843.*

49

The new novel was not popular. Its plot was too poorly worked out, its theme of selfishness too obscure. Only in the characterization is there real magic. Perhaps most memorable is Mrs. Gamp, the drunken midwife, who is "dispoged" to drink:

> The face of Mrs. Gamp – the nose in particular – was somewhat red and swollen, and it was difficult to enjoy her society without becoming conscious of a smell of spirits. Like most persons who have attained to great eminence in their profession, she took to hers very kindly: in so much that . . . she went to a lying-in or laying-out with equal zest and relish.

> (*Martin Chuzzlewit*, Chapter 19)

The 1840s, known as the "hungry forties," were the bleakest decade of the century. The Corn Laws kept the price of food high, and poor women and laborers starved. There were riots and hay-burning. In Ireland, the failure of the potato crop caused untold misery. Dickens could read, in official reports, of child labor in the mines, and he could see the "miseries and horrors" of the homeless children in London. Friends, like the writer and philosopher Thomas Carlyle, had already noted "a seriousness which became prominent in his conversation and writings. He had already learned to look upon the world as a scene where it was everyone's duty to make the lot of the miserable many less miserable." Dickens wrote a set of angry poems attacking those who opposed reform. "The Fine Old English Gentleman" was one of them:

> The good old laws were garnished well with gibbets,
>   whips and chains,
> With fine old English penalties, and fine old English pains,
> With rebel heads, and seas of blood once hot in rebel
>   veins;
> For all these things were requisite to guard the rich old
>   gains
> Of the fine old English Tory times;
> Soon may they come again.

"By Jove how Radical I am getting," he wrote to Forster.
Dickens tried to help the plight of poor children. In

1843, he visited a Ragged School in London, supported by a charity that he admired:

> It was held in a low-roofed den, in a sickening atmosphere in the midst of taint and dirt and pestilence; with all the deadly sins let loose, howling and shrieking at the doors . . . the pupils sang, fought, danced, robbed each other, seemed possessed by legions of devils . . .

("A sleep to startle us," *Household Words*, 1852)

"I have seldom seen," he told his friend, "anything so shocking as the dire neglect of soul and body exhibited in these children." It was while he was in Manchester, speaking about the need for education of the poor, that he suddenly thought of a new way to attack a heartless society dominated by greed.

The Ragged School Movement, which provided crude, basic education for poor, homeless city children, attracted Dickens's charitable attention.

In this John Leech illustration, Scrooge is visited by the ghost of his partner, Jacob Marley. His chain is made of ledgers and cash boxes, which represent his obsession with business and his neglect of suffering fellow creatures.

Dickens wrote the resulting story, *A Christmas Carol*, with furious speed and, as the corrections to the manuscript show, intense care. As he created Scrooge and Tiny Tim, he "walked about the black streets of London fifteen and twenty miles many a night." He "wept and laughed and wept again" at his own ideas. By Christmas 1843, *A Christmas Carol* was on sale and was at once "a prodigious success – the greatest, I think, I have ever achieved." Dickens had won back his public. John Forster remembered how "there poured upon him daily all through that Christmas time, letters from complete strangers . . . of which the general burden was to tell him . . . how the Carol had come to be read aloud there and was to be kept upon a little shelf by itself, and was to do them no end of good."

Dickens implanted his serious message in his brilliant blend of supernatural fantasy, pathos and comedy. Scrooge is the "economic man" of the 1840s, concerned only with business and profit and cut off from love and charity. His conversion by the three ghosts of his past, the present and his possible future is a carefully worked out allegory about society itself and its need to change its attitudes. A key message is given by the Ghost of Christmas Present, who shows Scrooge two city children "yellow, meagre, scowling, wolfish":

> "This boy is Ignorance. This girl is Want. Beware them both, and all of their degree, but most of all beware this boy, for on his brow I see that written which is Doom . . ."
> "Have they no refuge or resource?" cried Scrooge.
> "Are there no prisons?" said the Spirit, turning on him for the last time with his own words. "Are there no workhouses?"

(*A Christmas Carol*, Stave three)

Another Leech illustration: The Spirit of Christmas Yet To Come shows Scrooge the overgrown, neglected grave to which he will be condemned unless he changes his ways.

4

Boz the Universal

A Maclise sketch of Dickens reading his story The Chimes *aloud to his friends, including John Forster (left).*

A Christmas Carol did not completely free Dickens from the money worries that constantly beset him. He now planned to live for a year in Italy, saving expense by sub-letting his London home. In a "huge old coach," his family crossed Europe and settled in Genoa, where

54

Dickens was enchanted by the "awful, solemn, impenetrable blue" of the sea, seen from his villa, and "such green, green, green as flutters in the vineyard down below."

It was the disturbing, clashing bells from Genoa's churches that gave him the idea for another Christmas story, *The Chimes*. This was an angrier story than the *Carol*. "The Chimes," he claimed, "has a grip upon the very throat of the time." He returned to London to see the story through the press and read it aloud to a group of close friends.

Back in Italy, Dickens took his family for a tour of the country, sending home sketches of his travels later published as *Pictures from Italy*. Despite some powerful moments, and its illustrations by the artist Samuel Palmer, it was not an impressive book. Robert Browning, the poet, who knew Italy intimately, considered he had "gone on hurriedly, seeing and describing less and less." Yet it has powerful moments such as this description of a public execution in Rome:

> The young man kneeled down below the knife. His neck fitting into a hole made for the purpose, in a cross plank, was shut down by another plank above; exactly like the pillory. Immediately below him was a leather bag. And into it his head rolled instantly. The executioner was holding it by the hair, and walking with it round the scaffold showing it to the people, before one quite knew that the knife had fallen heavily, and with a rattling sound. There was a good deal of blood. When we left the window and went close up to the scaffold, it was very dirty. A strange appearance was the apparent annihilation of the neck . . . .
>
> (*Pictures from Italy*)

When he returned to England in May 1845, Dickens was invited to edit the *Daily News*, a new national newspaper. It would serve the cause of Liberal reform against the *Times*, which supported Conservatism. Despite his friends' misgivings, he accepted the post with enthusiasm. The paper appeared in January 1846, Dickens's first editorial advocating the "principles of progress and improvement" that the "advancing spirit of the times requires." The paper eventually flourished,

but its editor lasted for only seventeen days. He was irritated by the routine, the long hours and the long discussions. "Dickens was not a good editor," noted one of his staff, W.H. Russell.

Admitting the *Daily News* post was "a brief mistake," Dickens decided to live abroad again. He went to Switzerland, renting a house near Lausanne, overlooking Lake Geneva. On its balcony were "roses enough to smother the whole establishment of the *Daily News*."

He now began a new story in parts, *Dombey and Son*. He told Forster of his difficulties in starting without the stimulus of London. He regretted "the absence of streets and numbers of figures. I can't express how much I want these. It seems as if they supplied something to my brain which it cannot bear to lose . . . the toil and labour of writing day after day, without that magic lantern is immense!"

Dickens's novels from *Chuzzlewit* onward show careful planning. The novel form was evolving, and he now began to have serious rivals: his friend W.M. Thackeray's *Vanity Fair*, the Brontë sisters' *Jane Eyre* and *Wuthering Heights* would appear in 1847. Each of his books now had a "central idea," which, said his publisher, he "revolved in his mind until he had thought the matter thoroughly out." Then he prepared notes: ". . . a programme of his story with the characters. Finally, he took upon this skeleton and gave it literary sinew, blood and life."

In *Dombey*, Dickens intended to "do with Pride what its predecessor (*Chuzzlewit*) had done with Selfishness." Dombey's pride is based in his harsh business ambitions:

The earth was made for Dombey and Son to trade in, and the sun and the moon were made to give them light. Rivers and seas were formed to float their ships . . . winds blew for or against their enterprises: stars and planets circled in their orbits to preserve inviolate a system of which they were the centre . . . A.D. had no concern with Anno Domini but stood for Anno Dombei – and Son.

(*Dombey and Son*, Chapter 1)

His pride also lies in "manly" values. He sees his son as the continuation of his House's name; he has no real

Opposite *While he was in Rome, Dickens watched a public execution by guillotine. He remembered this horror in* A Tale of Two Cities, *where Sydney Carton (seen here in a still from the 1957 movie) goes to his death.*

THE TIMES
CHRONICLE
STANDARD HERALD
SUN
GLOBE
WALMSLEY

A cartoon of Dickens as editor of The Daily News. *Seen as a jackdaw among peacocks, he is watched by jealous eyes.*

affection for him. Florence, his loving daughter, is ignored. When Paul dies (in a scene that greatly affected Victorian readers), and when his business collapses, he finds that "his only staff and treasure . . . will be this neglected daughter." He comes to see that "Dombey and Son is indeed a daughter after all."

Dickens was the first author to comprehend the modern city and its life. London here is a "wild wilderness" full of "the rising clash and roar of the day's struggle." It is a destructive giant, in which an individual's misery is "as a drop of water in the sea, or as a grain of sand on the shore." Florence watches

Doré's picture of the railroad architecture dwarfing the houses of poor Londoners echoes the themes of Dombey and Son.

Railroad works at Westminster. In Dombey and Son, *the new railroads symbolize the ruthless force of industrial progress.*

stragglers tramping into town, "food for hospitals, the churchyards, the prisons, the river, fever, madness, vice and death, – they passed on to the monster, roaring in the distance and were lost." Dickens took the new railroads, now tearing their way ruthlessly through the city, as a symbol of the aggressive lack of care of which Dombey is a reflection. The railroad is "the triumphant monster Death . . . The power that forced itself upon

Personal History and Experience of David Copperfield — Nº VII

Chapter XIX.

I look about me, and make a discovery.

... save the way with ...
Do agnes
Do, mrs strong
Peggotty and Steerforth ...

first fall in love — *Play.*

Waiter

chapter XX.

Steerforth's Home.

Mrs Steerforth
Miss Dartle. "Then a hammer at her?"
"Eh? But is it really though? I meant ...

Chapter XXI.

Little Em'ly.

The Servant. Littimer.

Little Em'ly at Mr Omer's — Mr Omer "Jns parties"
Steerforth
Mr Barkis a ...

As the novel form became more sophisticated, and as novelist rivals sprang up in the late 1840s, Dickens's own work became more carefully planned. These detailed notes for Chapter 19 of David Copperfield are typical of the working methods of his maturity.

its iron way . : . defiant of all paths and roads, piercing through the heart of every obstacle, and dragging living creatures of all classes, ages and degrees behind it."

In the spring of 1848, when Dickens was back in London, a chance remark by Forster set him thinking about his early life.

Forster said that a friend of his had seen Dickens as a boy, working at Warren's Blacking. Dickens was

shocked at this uncovering of his secret past and said nothing. "I felt that I had unintentionally touched a painful place in his memory," said Forster. Some time later, Dickens sent Forster some pages from a projected autobiography: ". . . a picture of tragical suffering, and of tender as well as humorous fancy, unsurpassed in even the wonders of his published writing." Dickens was too disturbed by memory to continue. Instead he blended autobiographical fact into the fiction of *David Copperfield*.

At the beginning of 1849, Dickens's mind was "running like a high sea" about the new novel. He visited Yarmouth to find local color. At Forster's suggestion, he used a new form: first-person narration. This allows David, and Dickens, to relive and yet see in perspective the "slow agony" of his early life.

The novel also displays what Dickens called a "very complicated interweaving of truth and fiction." As a result, the early chapters, of which Dickens noted, "I seem to be sending some part of myself out into the Shadowy World," have extraordinary depth of feeling:

> I know that I worked, from morning until night, with common men and boys, a shabby child. I know that I lounged about the streets, insufficiently and unsatisfactorily fed. I know that but for the mercy of God, I might easily have been, for any care that was taken of me, a little robber or a little vagabond.

(*David Copperfield*, Chapter 11)

This powerful re-creation of a child's vision makes the opening of *David Copperfield* "a great English autobiography," comparable to William Wordsworth's majestic poem, *The Prelude*, published at this time.

Autobiographical elements are also woven into the rest of the novel. David's struggle to success, his self-denial, patience and endurance – which are contrasted with the weakness or selfishness of the other fatherless children in the book, Steerforth, Emily, Uriah Heep – are like Dickens's own fight for survival. He takes pride in "a patient and continuous energy which then began to be matured within me."

Opposite *David Copperfield is tormented by the cruel teacher, Mr. Creakle (played in this 1970 movie by Laurence Olivier). David wears the notice as punishment for biting his stepfather while he was being thrashed by him.*

There, on looking back, I find the source of my success
. . . Whatever I have tried to do in life, I have tried with
all my heart to do well . . . in great aims and small, I
have always been thoroughly in earnest.

(*David Copperfield*, Chapter 42)

Less successful is his reconsideration of his relationship with Maria Beadnell as the comic, touching and ultimately ill-fated marriage of David and Dora. Forster admired Dickens's concern with "the purities of the home," shown in David's second marriage with the sister-like Agnes: ". . . the source of every noble aspiration I ever had"; but modern readers find this climax of the novel sentimental and unconvincing. The true force of the novel's theme of marriage lies in a repeated sentence: "There can be no disparity in marriage, like unsuitability of mind and purpose." Here, one suspects, Dickens's feelings were more truly engaged, as his own marriage began to come under strain at this time.

David Copperfield is outstanding for its characters. The feckless Micawber and his genteel wife were based on Dickens's own parents. They live in the shadow of creditors' threats:

At these times, Mr. Micawber would be transported with
grief and mortification, even to the length (as I was once
made aware by a scream from his wife) of making
motions at himself with a razor; but within half an hour
afterwards, he would polish up his shoes with
extraordinary pains, and go out, humming a tune with
a greater air of gentility than ever.

(*David Copperfield*, Chapter 11)

"Of all my books, I like this the best," wrote Dickens in a later preface. "Like many fond parents, I have in my heart of hearts a favourite child. And his name is DAVID COPPERFIELD." The book became a general favorite. The poet Matthew Arnold, praising the novel for its portrait of the Victorian middle class, exclaimed, "What treasures of gaiety, invention, life! . . . What alertness and resources! What a soul of good nature and kindness governing the whole."

5
The Critic
of Society

Early in 1850, Dickens decided to return to journalism. He had always been attracted to the magazine format. Better printing methods and easier distribution now made such a project more likely to be profitable. *Household Words*, published weekly, was like the literary miscellanies he had admired as a boy: part entertainment, with stories and poems, part instruction, with articles about "social wonders, good and evil." It campaigned for social reforms of all kinds. Well-known authors such as Elizabeth Gaskell and Charles Reade, and the newcomer Wilkie Collins, contributed stories.

Above all, there was Dickens with his keenly observed commentaries on the sufferings of the poor. He went to see the homeless in Whitechapel:

> Crouched against the wall of the Workhouse, in the dark street, on the muddy pavement-stones, with the rain raining upon them, were five bundles of rags. They were motionless, and had no resemblance to the human form. Five great beehives, covered with rags – five dead bodies taken out of graves, tied neck and heels, and covered with rags – would have looked like those five bundles upon which the rain rained down in the public street.

("A nightly scene in London," 1856)

Sometimes Dickens used his powerful rhetoric in angry attacks on the government:

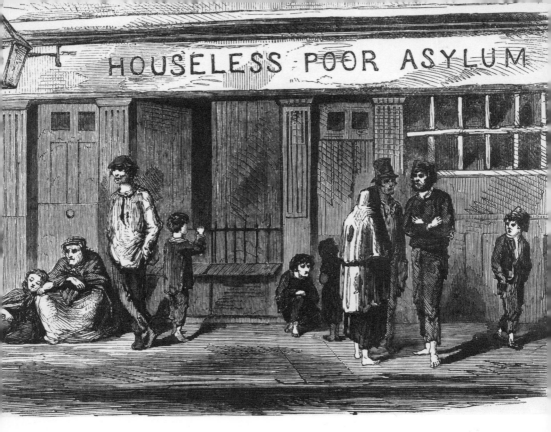

HOUSELESS POOR ASYLUM

I saw a Minister of State sitting in his closet; and, round about him, rising from the country which he governed, up to the Eternal Heavens, was a low dull howl of Ignorance. It was a wild, inexplicable mutter, confused but full of threatening . . . I saw thirty thousand children, hunted, flogged, imprisoned, but not taught – who might have been nurtured by the wolf or bear, so little of humanity had they – all joining in this doleful cry.

("A December vision," 1856)

In his magazine Household Words, *Dickens wrote angrily about the sufferings of the poor. Here, homeless people wait outside a London workhouse, an illustration from Henry Mayhew's study of the city's poor.*

When the lease of Devonshire Terrace expired, Dickens had to find a new home. In November 1851, the family moved into a town mansion in Tavistock Square, Bloomsbury. As usual, with his fanatical attention to detail, Dickens supervised all the conversion and decoration, joyfully finding that the children's schoolroom was large enough to contain a stage. He was passionately fond of amateur dramatics and had formed a company of friends to act in plays for charity, even performing before Queen Victoria.

He now had eight children, and another was born in 1852. He was an affectionate father while the children were young, at his best at Christmas, leading the dancing and running the conjuring for his oldest son's birthday party on Twelfth Night. He was also the lively organizer of games, walks and swimming on the regular family vacations at Broadstairs in Kent. Dickens, said a guest, "warmed the social atmosphere with that summerglow which seemed to attend him." Yet with his obsession for order and punctuality, he was beginning to be a domestic tyrant, too. Each morning Dickens toured the house to check that all was in order. "If a chair was out of place or a blind not quite straight, or a crumb left on the floor, woe betide the offender," said his daughter Mamie.

In the 1850s, Dickens, like other social critics, became impatient with outdated institutions of government that no longer suited the needs of an industrial society. Always contemptuous of the law – "grinding Jack's bones to make its bread" – he joined others in condemning the Court of Chancery, described by a *Times* writer as "a name of terror, a devastating gulf, a den whence no footsteps return." The delays and huge costs of cases there absorbed fortunes and ruined lives.

Chancery is at the center of *Bleak House*. Out of the imaginary case of Jarndyce vs. Jarndyce, there unfolds an impressive panorama of mid-Victorian society and its corruptions. The haunting opening makes a dense London fog a symbol of the guilt and confusion created by the Court:

Fog everywhere. Fog up the river, where it flows among green cuts and meadows; fog down the river, where it rolls defiled among the tiers of shipping, and the waterside pollutions of a great (and dirty) city . . . At the very heart of the fog, sits the Lord High Chancellor in his High Court of Chancery . . .

(*Bleak House*, Chapter 1)

The Court spreads its web from the aristocratic mansion, Chesney Wold, to the deadly city slum, Tom–all–Alone's, the decay and disease of which are a threat to the whole of society:

A portrait of Dickens in 1849.

These ruined shelters have bred a crowd of foul existence that crawls in and out of gaps in walls and boards and coils itself to sleep in maggot numbers, where the rain drips in; and comes and goes, fetching and carrying fever, and sowing more evil in its every footprint than Lord Coodle, and Sir Thomas Noodle, and the Duke of Foodle, and all the fine gentlemen in office, down to Zoodle, shall set right in five hundred years.

(*Bleak House*, Chapter 16)

To encompass his criticism of society, and to tell the story in *Bleak House*, Dickens uses two narrators. The first-person narrative of the gentle Esther Summerson is contained within a third-person, omniscient (all-seeing and all-knowing) narrative. This voice uses the present tense to give a sense of immediacy to descriptions and events, and it has often been seen as Dickens's own, as it protests against the corruptions of Chancery, the abuses of charity and the failure of responsibility in society. This part of the narrative angrily announces the death of Jo, the orphan crossing sweeper, who is a representative victim of society's neglect and indifference:

The light is come upon the dark benighted way. Dead! Dead, your Majesty. Dead, my lords and gentlemen. Dead, Right Reverends and Wrong Reverends of every order. Dead, men and women, born with Heavenly compassion in your hearts. And dying thus around us every day.

(*Bleak House*, Chapter 48)

Esther's narrative is limited, in its perceptions, to the facts of her own experience. However, her growing understanding reveals the ills of Chancery; she sees it destroy the happiness and waste the lives of loved ones and strangers alike. Esther's practical goodness, like that of her guardian, John Jarndyce, stands in sharp contrast to the self-delusions, irresponsibility and exploitativeness displayed by many of those she meets.

Opposite *A scene from* Bleak House: *Jo, the crossing sweeper, shows Lady Dedlock the grave of her secret lover in an obscure London churchyard.*

In his next novel, Dickens recalled the horror he had felt in 1838, when he first visited the Manchester cotton mills. In 1853, he went back to Lancashire to observe a hard-fought strike in mills in Preston. A year

later, he began work on *Hard Times*, a satire on the dehumanizing effects of industrialism and of extreme expressions of the Utilitarian philosophy. This philosophy, which had originally aspired to realize "the greatest happiness for the greatest number," became, in the view of Dickens and many others, distorted by its own materialism, which underestimated the value of imagination and saw human beings as mere statistics.

Hard Times does not advocate violent action, or even political reform. It urges the most accessible revolution, that of the human change of heart. This is a revolution of education and sympathy and was, for Dickens, the necessary basis of reform.

Dickens's sympathies were for the industrial working people as fellow humans. He aimed his attack at those who seemed to forget the humanity of working people: the industrial employers, and those who strove to put Utilitarian ideas into practice. "My satire is against those who see figures and averages, and nothing else," he wrote. *Hard Times* attacks these people and ideas with its use of wonder and fantasy.

In Hard Times, *Dickens condemned the inhuman life of Victorian factory workers. Even women and children were exploited as cheap labor.*

Coketown, the industrial city of *Hard Times*, is inhuman: ". . . a town of unnatural red and black like the painted face of a savage." "Shrouded in a haze of its own," it is dominated by a river "that ran purple with ill-smelling dye," by "the stifling smell of hot oil," the "whirr of shafts and wheels," and the tireless steam engines whose pistons go up and down like the head of "melancholy mad elephants." The city is controlled by pitiless "steam-engine intellects." Here, the imagination of schoolchildren is crushed under the instruction "Never wonder," and the individuality of the working man – glimpsed in the story of Stephen Blackpool – is crushed in the hostilities between employer and trade union. Stephen's dilemma highlights that of working people who are remote from both their rulers and their union representatives. Lacking justice and guidance, they are unable to communicate with their masters and are prey to the persuasive power of political agitators.

The nightmarish ugliness and pollution of the Victorian industrial town is represented in Dickens's Coketown, dominated by smoking chimneys and the sound of factory machines.

Thomas Carlyle, in his essay "Chartism," had warned that the "bitter discontent" of oppressed working people was an "inward fire" which, "grown fierce and mad," could "flash up from time to time," demanding reform. The fire metaphor is central to *Hard Times*. Here, however, it has a double meaning. It stands for the oppressions of industrialism, reflected in the red brick, red smoke and red faces of the Coketown workers. In addition, fire imagery stands for suppressed passion and emotion in the individual, particularly in the character of Louisa Gradgrind:

> . . . yet struggling through the dissatisfaction of her face, there was a light with nothing to rest upon, a fire with nothing to burn, a starved imagination keeping life in itself somehow.

> (*Hard Times*, Chapter 3)

Dickens was on vacation near Boulogne in France when the Crimean War began in 1854. He shared in the general early enthusiasm for the war and was full of "admiration of our valiant men," whom he watched at drill with their French allies nearby. His mood soon changed when he read W.H. Russell's *Times* reports from the Crimea during the hard winter of 1854–55. By Christmas, more than two-thirds of the 54,000 men of the British army there were reported dead – of wounds, sickness and neglect. Like many others, Dickens blamed the ineffective bureaucrats of the War Office for the confusion in supplies for the army. "We have got involved in meshes of aristocratic red-tape to our unspeakable confusion, loss and sorrow," he complained, and he joined in the protest to demand administrative reform.

One strand of *Little Dorrit*, begun in 1855, is its satire of government bureaucracy:

> The Circumlocution Office was . . . the most important Department under Government . . . Its finger was in the largest public pie, and in the smallest public tart. Whatever was required to be done, the Circumlocution Office was beforehand with all the public departments in the art of perceiving – HOW NOT TO DO IT.

> (*Little Dorrit*, Chapter 10)

Opposite *In* Little Dorrit, *Dickens re-created the stifling world of the Marshalsea Prison, where his own father had been held for debt. On this original title-page,* Little Dorrit *enters the prison, where she has lived all her life.*

74

LITTLE DORRIT

BY

CHARLES DICKENS

LONDON:

BRADBURY & EVANS, BOUVERIE STREET

1857.

This is only part of Dickens's picture of a society full of sinister secrets, fallen into the hands of the self-seeking bureaucrats, the Tite Barnacles, or the fraudulent financial speculator, Mr. Merdle. The novel's closely observed picture of the Marshalsea Prison, and the shadow of its spiked wall, reflects the wider concept of society itself as a huge prison in which people are trapped by ambition or greed.

If Little Dorrit herself is too sentimental a character for our taste, Dickens showed his mature powers in the delicate, pathetic portrait of the debtor William Dorrit, a victim of financial corruption, whose shame makes his "irresolute hands nervously wander to his trembling lip" and whose foolish pride delights in his dubious status as "Father of the Marshalsea."

Dickens's increasing restlessness, which made him "a monster to my family, a dread phenomenon to myself," now created unease in his marriage. It began with a play. As Dickens's friendship with Forster faded, he became closer to the younger novelist Wilkie Collins, who became his companion in "theatrical and other lounging evenings" and "low-life jaunts." In 1856, Collins wrote a melodrama, *The Frozen Deep*, based on Sir John Franklin's ill-fated Arctic expedition. Dickens took the part of an explorer who saved his rival in love and died in the arms of the woman who had rejected him. At the London performances, Collins was impressed by the power of Dickens's acting: "He literally electrified the audience." When the play moved to Manchester, Frances Ternan, a professional actress, and her daughters, Ellen and Maria, were hired to take parts. Ellen, eighteen, fair-haired and blue-eyed, at once fascinated Dickens. He fell in love with her and, for the rest of his life, tried to make her the "one friend and companion I never made . . . The one happiness I have missed."

Dickens's marriage collapsed. In letters to Forster, he confessed his alienation from Catherine, who had grown stout and, in his eyes, dull, after years of child-bearing. "Poor Catherine and I are not made for each other, and there's no help for it. It is not only that she makes me uneasy and unhappy but that I make her so too." As her husband became more involved with his secret life with Ellen, Catherine, who moved to a separate home, remained silent.

Opposite *Little Dorrit, born in the Marshalsea Prison, is haunted by the shadow of its bars and its spiked wall. This is a still from the 1987 movie.*

Above *Dickens loved acting. Here (lying, center) he plays the part of an Arctic explorer in Wilkie Collins's 1856 melodrama* The Frozen Deep.

This marriage crisis coincided with another change of home. In 1855, he had seen that Gad's Hill Place, "literally the dream of my childhood," was for sale. He decided to buy it. The house, wrote Dickens, was "old-fashioned, plain and comfortable with a noble prospect looking down into the valley of the Medway." In May 1857, after extensive alterations had been carried out, he celebrated his move with some of his friends. The children, much shaken by their parents' separation, still lived with their father. They were presided over by their aunt, the kindly, serene Georgina Howarth.

The young actress, Ellen Ternan, with whom Dickens fell in love. He called her "The one happiness I have missed."

The romantic self-sacrifice of his part in *The Frozen Deep* gave Dickens his first idea for *A Tale of Two Cities*. A quarrel with his publishers ended *Household Words*, but a new Dickens magazine, *All The Year Round*, appeared in April 1859, with the new serial as centerpiece. "The best story I have ever written" soon caught the public imagination.

Dickens used a French source for his story, blending into it careful research from the literature of the French Revolution of 1789. His friend Thomas Carlyle's "wonderful book" on the subject was a particular inspiration. Contemporary horrors from the 1857 Indian Mutiny also affected him. Dickens shows how violence bred by years of "unspeakable suffering, intolerable oppression, and heartless indifference" in France destroys the innocent and the guilty alike. In the execution of Foulon, who once told starving peasants to eat grass, Dickens at once warns against violence and shows his fascination with it:

Now, on his knees; now, on his feet; now, on his back; dragged and struck at, and stifled by the bunches of grass and straw that were thrust into his face by hundreds of hands; torn, bruised, panting, bleeding, he was hauled to the nearest street corner . . . then the rope was merciful, and held him, and his head was soon upon a pike, with grass enough in the mouth . . .

(*A Tale of Two Cities*, Book 2, Chapter 22)

This is the shortest, least decorated of Dickens's novels. Its intensity is quickly created in the bold patterns of its opening sentence:

It was the best of times, it was the worst of times, it was the age of wisdom, it was the age of foolishness . . . it was the season of Light, it was the season of Darkness, it was the spring of hope, it was the winter of despair . . .

These patterns of opposites in place and theme also tie the novel together: London contrasts with Paris; the ideals of the revolution with its horrible methods; the idea of changing society and that of changing the self; death and rebirth; guilt and redemption. There are contrasts among the characters, too. So Miss Pross, Lucy's

Opposite *A cartoon mocking Dickens's pious statements about his broken marriage. The wedding ring is related to the title of his new magazine,* All The Year Round, *which was started after an argument with his publishers caused the closure of* Household Words.

The hysteria and violence of the French Revolution are vividly portrayed in A Tale of Two Cities, *which Dickens called "the best story I have ever written."*

heroic companion, counterbalances the monstrous Madame Defarge – the mother of love and the mother of blood. The conventional hero Charles Darnay and the dissolute Sydney Carton are also opposed. Twins in appearance, they both love Lucy. In his self-sacrifice on the scaffold, Carton redeems himself and saves Darnay for Lucy. His last words have moved countless thousands of readers:

> It is a far, far better thing that I do than I have ever done; it is a far, far better rest that I go to than I have ever known.

(*A Tale of Two Cities*, Book 3, Chapter 15)

6

The National Sparkler

The Dickens family was not always happy in its new home. The children, who had once seemed so wonderful, disappointed their father as they grew up. He was fond of his daughters, Kate and Mamie, but the boys, crushed by their father's personality and without any of his genius, seemed tiresome: "The house is pervaded by boys and every boy has an unaccountable and awful power of producing himself in every part of the house at every moment, apparently in fourteen pairs of creaking boots." "Why," asked Dickens in a letter, "did the kings in the fairy tales want children?" Only Henry, who became a successful lawyer, pleased him. The others were packed off into the armed services or abroad. The oldest, Charley, concluded sadly that "the children of my father's brain were much more real to him at times than we were."

Dickens's downstairs study at Gad's Hill looked across his handsome gardens. On his desk were his knick-knacks without which he could not write: the bronze fighting frogs, the man with puppies in his pockets. Grip, a stuffed pet raven, sat nearby. Dummy books with comic titles – *Hansard's Guide to Refreshing Sleep, History of a Short Chancery Suit, 21 vols, Malthus's Nursery Songs* – were stuck to the doorback. There were mirrors everywhere, to give light, because Dickens was vain and because he used his reflection to help create his characters. Later he also used a small Swiss chalet, given to him by an actor friend, as a writing room. He loved to

Above *Dickens (right, lying down) with family and friends at Gad's Hill Place near Rochester, which he bought in 1856. He had admired the house during the Chatham phase of his boyhood.*

Opposite *Dickens writing in his study at Gad's Hill Place. He was obsessively orderly and could not write without his desk knick-knacks before him.*

entertain, and guests shared the dancing, garden sports, memory games and charades he delighted in. Conversation at table was not profound. Dickens liked to hear about ghosts, hypnotism, the latest murder. For leisure he took tremendous walks, striding along at four miles an hour. One guest confessed to being "utterly spent and exhausted" by trying to keep up with him.

It was perhaps his walks into the marshes near Rochester that gave Dickens the first idea for *Great Expectations*. It is interesting to compare the story of Pip, the poor boy made rich by the convict Magwitch, with *David Copperfield*. Dickens himself saw the similarity and told Forster he had read over the earlier novel to avoid "unconscious repetitions." Both novels had strong autobiographical elements, but *Great Expectations* uses these more subtly and indirectly.

The graves of the Comport children in Cooling churchyard near Rochester. Dickens saw these graves during walks as a boy and used them in the opening of Great Expectations.

David is an innocent whom the world torments, yet he battles against odds to win prosperity and a fulfilling marriage. From the first, Pip is seen as a guilt-ridden being, whose easily won success in becoming a gentleman of leisure is eventually exposed to himself and the world as a hollow sham.

Great Expectations is one of the great books in the nineteenth-century tradition of the *bildungsroman*: a story of growing up, of an individual, of the formation of character. Dickens skillfully balances the immediacy of young Pip's reactions with the wisdom of the older Pip's narrative. This is a man who has learned from his experience, and Dickens preserves Pip's integrity by allowing him insights, self-criticism, honesty and irony throughout the narrative. Dickens's own embarrassed relationship with his father may lie behind the book's exploration of Pip's relationships with a number of parent-figures. Pip is an orphan, but he acquires many substitute parents: the convict who leaps from the graves, in the book's dramatic opening, like his father reborn; the kindly Joe; his harsh sister; the mysterious, eccentric Miss Havisham; the powerful lawyer,

Pip is terrified when he meets the convict Abel Magwitch, who will change his life. A still from the 1946 movie Great Expectations.

Mr. Jaggers. Pip betrays Joe but comes to see the worth of his loving kindness. He fears and despises Magwitch but comes to love and care for him as he dies. There are more precious things in life, he discovers, than "being a gentleman."

Crime, always a passionate concern of Dickens, is a key theme. There is the convict: ". . . a fearful man, all in coarse grey, with a great iron on his leg." Moored on the river is the sinister prison hulk, "like a wicked Noah's Ark," where convicts are kept before transportation. There are the casts of hanged men in Jagger's office: ". . . faces peculiarly swollen, and twitchy about the nose." Outside Newgate Prison is a man in mildewed clothes that "he had bought cheap of the executioner." There is the deeply moving court scene when Magwitch and thirty other prisoners are sentenced to death together. The raindrops on the windows are like tears of mourning:

> The whole scene starts out again in the vivid colours of the moment, down to the drops of April rain on the windows of the court, glittering in the rays of April sun. Penned in the dock . . . were two and thirty men and women; some defiant, some stricken with terror, some sobbing and weeping, some covering their faces, some staring gloomily about . . . The sun was striking in at the great windows of the court, through the glittering drops of rain upon the glass, and it made a broad shaft of light between the two and thirty and the judge, linking both together, and perhaps reminding some . . . how both were passing on . . . to the greater judgement that knoweth all things and cannot err.

> (*Great Expectations*, Chapter 56)

Yet Dickens is also saying that moral crimes – pride, ambition, self-deception, cruelty, snobbery – are more destructive than legal crimes. Pip moves from his contempt for Joe and the convict, and from his obsessive love for the cruel Estella, to a position where he can understand and reject his false values.

This idea of Pip's spiritual progress makes the novel's original, but later abandoned, ending impressive. This imagined a complete break with Estella and a final meeting, as strangers, years later:

The lady and I looked sadly enough on one another . . .
I was very glad afterwards to have had the interview:
for, in her face and in her voice, and in her touch, she
gave me the assurance that suffering had been stronger
than Miss Havisham's teaching, and had given her a
heart to understand what my heart used to be . . .

(*Great Expectations*, Manuscript)

*The eccentric Miss
Havisham has worn
her wedding dress ever
since she was jilted
just before her
marriage. She
encourages Pip to fall
in love with her ward,
the heartless Estella.*

Forster, like many readers today, found that conclusion
"more consistent with the drift, as well as the actual
working out, of the tale," and better than the sentimental, if ambigious ending, pressed on Dickens by his
novelist friend, Edward Bulwer Lytton:

. . . the evening mists were rising now, and in all the
broad expanse of tranquil light they showed to me, I
saw no shadow of another parting from her.

(*Great Expectations*, Chapter 59: final 1868 revision)

Besides the profound exploration of Pip, Dickens's characterization is at its most inventive and grotesque in this novel. We know the dominating Mr. Jaggers before we see him, by his threatening office where "the clients seemed to have had a habit of backing up against the wall; the wall, especially opposite Mr. Jaggers' chair, being greasy with shoulders." There is Miss Havisham, based on a real eccentric Dickens had seen as a child. She still wears her decaying wedding dress years after her rejection at the altar. Her rotting wedding feast, still set out, expresses the moral decay of her obsessed mind:

> A centrepiece of some kind was in the middle of this cloth . . . It was so heavily overhung with cobwebs that its form was quite indistinguishable: and, as I looked along the yellow expanse out of which I remember it seeming to grow like a black fungus, I saw speckledlegged spiders with blotchy bodies running home to it, and running out from it.

> (*Great Expectations*, Chapter 11)

Pip is spoiled by the riches from his mysterious "Great Expectations." Money is also a theme of *Our Mutual Friend*, begun in 1864. London, "such a bleak shrill city, such a hopeless city with no rent in the leaden canopy of its sky," is the center of a money-mad society. Dickens borrowed a strange item from a newspaper, about a dustman who had made a fortune from his heaps of rubbish, to make his central point: money is filth. Money distorts values and misdirects efforts; money kills. In an experimental novel that uses several writing styles, Dickens employs a chorus of "Voices of Society" to underline his message and his attacks on the money-mad Podsnaps, Veneerings and Lammles:

> Where does he come from? Shares. Where is he going to? Shares. What are his tastes? Shares. Has he any principles? Shares. What squeezes him into Parliament? Shares. Perhaps he never of himself achieved success in anything, never originated anything, never produced anything! Sufficient answer to all; Shares. O Mighty Shares!

> (*Our Mutual Friend*, Book 1, Chapter 10)

Always fascinated by the Thames, "the great black river with its dreary shores," Dickens uses it here as a connecting thread in the narrative, and as an impressive symbol of death and rebirth. Most of the novel's memorable scenes involve the river. In the somber opening, Lizzie Hexham's father drifts on the water at night looking for the corpses from which he makes a gruesome living.

A "Found drowned" poster disguises the actual fate of the central character, John Harman, who lives under an assumed name to test the strange terms of his father's will. Old Betty Higden, escaping from the horror of the workhouse, dies beside the river; and Lizzie's jealous

lover, Bradley Headstone, attacks his rival, Eugene Wrayburn, on its brink, leaving "a bloody face turned up towards the moon and drifting away . . ."

Although Dickens condemned the power of money in his fiction, he never lost his relentless concern to accumulate wealth. With so many demands on his purse, he could not relax his efforts. In the 1860s he developed a quick way to earn ready money: by public readings from his work.

Although he had read for charity in 1853, he began his regular tours in 1858, traveling around Britain, and to Paris. He carefully managed every detail: there was a specially-made reading desk and gas lighting placed to illuminate his face. He dressed with great care; the flowers – even the fallen petals – from his buttonhole became cherished souvenirs. He prepared prompt scripts, cutting description and adding dialogue. Under-linings and margin notes guided the emphasis. His repertoire was based mostly on his early drama-influenced novels: the trial of Pickwick, *Nicholas Nickleby*, the storm in *David Copperfield*, the death of Paul Dombey. A late story, "Dr. Marigold's Prescriptions," was written for the readings. It is a masterly piece of Victorian comedy and sentiment.

A Christmas Carol was a favorite from first to last. An observer described the astonishing force of his acting: "The power of facial expression is wonderful . . . He gives a distinct voice to each character . . . At one moment he is savage old Scrooge, at the next, his jolly nephew, and, in the twinkling of an eye, little timid, lisping Bob Cratchit appears." His magnetic stage presence – his extraordinary eyes, his expressive hands – captivated everyone. "I had no conception," said his friend Thomas Carlyle, "what capacities lie in the human face and voice. No theatre-stage could have had more players than seemed to flit about his face." It was not simply a reading but a re-creation of the novels. The readings brought Dickens both profit and intense satisfaction: "There's nothing in the world equal to seeing the house rise to you, one sea of delightful faces, one hurrah of applause!"

Yet reading was exhausting and helped speed the decline in Dickens's health. The 1865 Staplehurst railroad disaster was another blow. He was returning from France with Ellen Ternan in June when the train was

Opposite *The brilliant readings from his works that marked the last part of Dickens's career also ruined his health. This drawing by Harry Furniss shows him shattered by a reading of the murder of Nancy from* Oliver Twist. *Sikes and Nancy can be seen in the background.*

derailed on the Staplehurst viaduct. Dickens helped to rescue horribly injured people: ". . . twisted up among iron and wood, and mud and water." The crash was a ". . . horrible . . . terrible" reminder of death. Thereafter Dickens could not travel by rail without trembling and sweating. The brilliant, supernatural story "The Signalman" (1866) was one result of this horror.

Despite his declining health, Dickens now contemplated a reading tour of Australia. He finally settled on a return journey to the United States. In November 1867, he set off for Boston. The destruction of the Civil War, the swift pace of social change, the disappearance of the crude "yellow press" meant that the tactlessness of his first visit was forgotten and forgiven. Everywhere he went, he met ". . . success . . . beyond description." The writer John Greenleaf Whittier watched him read: "These marvelous characters of his come forth . . . as if their creator had breathed new life into them . . . You must beg, borrow, or steal a ticket and hear him. Another such star-shower is not to be expected in one's lifetime." Profits were enormous. One night in New York, his manager "put such an immense untidy heap of paper money on the table that it looked like a family wash." When he went home in April 1868, he took £20,000 profit, equivalent then to nearly $100,000. At a farewell banquet, Dickens put aside his past criticism: "Better for this globe to be riven by an earth-quake, fired by a comet than that it should present the spectacle of these two great nations . . . ever again being arrayed against each other."

Back at Gad's Hill, the "National Sparkler," as the press called him, prepared a sensational new reading item: Bill Sikes's murder of Nancy from *Oliver Twist*. "I have got something so horrible out of it that I am afraid to try it in public," he told a friend. At his first effort in private he noted that his guests were "unmistakably pale, and had horror-struck faces." A young friend, Edmund Yates, watched his public performance: "Gradually warming with excitement, he flung aside his book and acted the scene of the murder, shrieked the terrified pleadings of the girl, growled the brutal savagery of the murderer . . . there was not one but was astonished at the power and versatility of his genius." A *Times* critic said that "he has always trembled on the boundary line that separates the reader from the actor . . . Now he clears it by a leap." His doctors noted that the "murder" made his pulse-rate shoot up, and that after reading he would lie exhausted unable to speak for ten minutes. His tour of 1869 had to be concluded prematurely, yet, two days before his death, he was seen in his garden, re-creating the murder for himself.

Opposite *Dickens (center) was involved in the 1865 Staplehurst railroad disaster. The experience weakened his health but may have given him the inspiration for his railroad ghost story,* The Signalman.

In summer 1869, Dickens began his last novel, *The
Mystery of Edwin Drood*. Impressed by Wilkie Collins's
detective serial, *The Moonstone*, he set out to create something similar, linking England with the mysterious Far
East. John Jasper, choirmaster of Cloisterham, leads a
double life, traveling to London opium dens to satisfy
his addiction. Edwin is Jasper's nephew, engaged to
Rosa, whom Jasper loves. Edwin vanishes on Christmas
Eve after a thunderstorm. Did Jasper murder Edwin? Is
he actually dead? As the novel remained unfinished, no
one knows, although Luke Fildes, the illustrator,
claimed he had been told to draw Jasper strangling
Edwin with a long scarf.

The year 1870 began with Dickens's "Farewell Readings." Tired, numb down the left side and in pain, he
finished in March. "From these garish lights, I vanish
now for evermore, with a heartfelt, grateful, respectful
and affectionate farewell." Tears rolled down his cheeks.
At this time, too, he at last met Queen Victoria in private
audience.

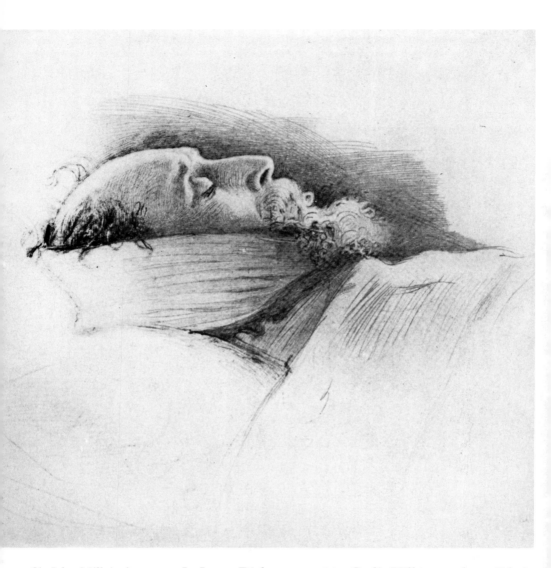

Sir John Millais drew this study of Dickens just after his death at Gad's Hill Place in June 1870.

In June, Dickens went to Gad's Hill to work on *Edwin Drood*. On Wednesday June 8, he worked all day in the chalet, finishing his episode with a flourish. At dinner with Georgina, he said he felt ill. He jumped up, saying he must go at once to London. Then he fell to the ground unconscious. He was lifted onto a sofa where he remained until Thursday evening. Then he sighed, a tear trickled down his cheek, and he died. His children, and Georgina and Ellen were beside him.

He had hoped to be buried in his beloved Rochester. The *Times* reflected public opinion in insisting on a grave in Poet's Corner in Westminster Abbey, London. For three days, an unending procession of people walked past the open grave, which was almost covered with flowers. It was a fitting tribute to England's greatest and most popular novelist.

Dickens's Dream *by Robert Buss shows Dickens in his study, surrounded by scenes and characters created from his extraordinary imagination.*

Glossary

Antipathy Dislike for someone.

Corn Laws Laws imposing a tax on imported corn, or grain, (from 1804 to 1846), to make it more expensive than that produced at home. In the 1840s, bad harvests and the Irish potato famine caused much protest against the Laws, which kept the price of bread artificially high.

Edwardian Referring to the time when Edward VII was king of England (1901–10).

Farce A comic play with a complicated plot including many misunderstandings and absurd situations.

First-person narration A story told by a character writing as "I."

Furore A strong outburst of protest or anger.

Genre A type of writing (i.e. novel, play, poem, etc.).

Hansard A detailed record of every word spoken in Parliamentary debates.

Laissez-faire An economic theory suggesting that the government should not interfere with the activities of individuals, especially in business affairs.

Malthus, Thomas (1766–1834). A theorist who studied population growth in relation to the economy. He considered that wages for laboring men should be kept low to prevent them from fathering children.

Materialism Thinking that puts things such as money and possessions before ideas or spiritual values.

Melodrama A play that is based on crude emotions, whether tragic or comic.

Miscellany A collection of various types of writing such as essays, poems, or stories; usually in a magazine.

Newgate novels Crime fiction popular in the 1830s. The writers treated crime with sympathy, blaming it on poverty.

New Poor Law The 1834 Law set up workhouses run by a "union" of parishes. The Law aimed to encourage work and to discourage living off charity. The system affected the old and very young badly, as *Oliver Twist* shows.

Part work Dickens published his novels in paper-bound parts, usually on a monthly basis. They then appeared in book form in the usual Victorian three-volume format.

Picaresque A story based on adventures and meetings during a journey.

Plot The intertwining of several stories within a novel.

Ragged school A simple school, provided by charity, offering basic education to city slum children.

Rhetoric Words and sentences arranged to make an impressive effect.

Satire The use of ridicule to·attack a fault or weakness in a person or society.

Symbol Something that represents or stands for something else.

Theme The general idea raised by a work of literature.

Tory The popular name for a member of the British Conservative Party.

Vagaries Rapidly changing fancies.

Victorian Referring to the time of Queen Victoria of England (1837–1901).

Yellow press The sensational popular press in the United States at the end of the nineteenth century. The term comes from a strip cartoon called "The Yellow Kid" in the *New York World*.

List of dates

Year	Life	Works
1812	February 7: Born in Portsmouth.	
1814	Dickens family move to London.	
1817	Family move to Chatham, Kent.	
1822	Family move to Camden Town, London.	
1823	John Dickens arrested for debt: placed in Marshalsea Prison.	
1823–24	Dickens at Warren's Blacking Factory.	
1824–27	Continues education at Wellington Academy, London.	
1827	Becomes solicitor's clerk.	
1828	Learns shorthand. Begins reporting at Doctors' Commons.	
1830	First meeting with Maria Beadnell. Continues self-education at British Museum.	
1832	Begins work with *Mirror of Parliament*.	
1833	Breaks with Maria Beadnell.	First published essay in *Monthly* Magazine.

1834	Reporter for *Morning Chronicle*. Used pen-name "Boz" for first time. Meets Catherine Hogarth.	
1835	Reporter covering political events across the country. Becomes engaged to Catherine.	
1836	Marriage to Catherine. Editor of *Bentley's Miscellany*. Friendship with John Forster begins. "Boz-mania" follows success of *Pickwick*. Gives up journalism.	*Sketches by Boz* 1836–37. *Pickwick Papers* 1836–37
1837	Birth of first child. Moves to Doughty Street. Sudden death of Mary Hogarth.	*Oliver Twist* 1837–39 (published in book form 1838).
1838	Enters fashionable London society.	*Nicholas Nickleby* 1838–39.
1839	Moves to Devonshire Terrace.	
1840		*Master Humphrey's Clock* includes *The Old Curiosity Shop* 1840–41
1841		*Barnaby Rudge*
1842	January-June: Tour of United States. Furor about his comments on US.	*American Notes*
1843		*Martin Chuzzlewit* 1843–44 *A Christmas Carol*.
1844	Lives in Genoa, Italy.	*The Chimes*.
1845	Tour of Italy and France.	*Cricket on the Hearth*.

1846	Editor of *Daily News*. Lives in Switzerland and Paris.	*Pictures from Italy*.
1847		Autobiographical fragment (for Forster) *Dombey and Son* 1847–48
1848		*The Haunted Man* (story)
1849		*David Copperfield* 1849–50
1850	Begins *Household Words*. Amateur drama company perform before Queen Victoria.	
1851	Moves to Tavistock Square. Death of John Dickens.	
1852		*Bleak House* 1852–53
1854		*Hard Times*
1855	Meets Maria Beadnell again. Lives in Paris for six months.	*Little Dorrit* 1855–57
1856	Buys Gad's Hill Place.	
1857	Acts in *The Frozen Deep*. Meets Ellen Ternan. First public reading in London. Moves to Gad's Hill Place.	
1858	Separation from wife. Statement on this in *Household Words*. First reading tour.	*Reprinted Pieces* (essays from *Household Words*)
1859	Editor of *All The Year Round*.	*A Tale of Two Cities*
1860	Continues readings throughout decade.	*Great Expectations* 1860–61

1861		*The Uncommercial Traveller* (essays from *All The Year Round)*
1864		*Our Mutual Friend* 1864–65
1865	Involved in Staplehurst railroad disaster. Health deteriorates.	
1867–68	Second American tour: huge success.	
1869	First public reading of murder of Nancy from *Oliver Twist*.	*The Mystery of Edwin Drood* 1869–70 (unfinished)
1870	Farewell readings in London. Audience with Queen Victoria. June 9: dies at Gad's Hill Place aged 58. June 14: Buried in Poet's Corner, Westminster Abbey.	

Further Reading

The works

The novels are published in hardcover and paperback by several publishers.

The Oxford Illustrated Dickens: Complete Works, 21 volumes (Oxford, reissued 1987)

COLLINS, P. (ed.) *Sikes and Nancy* (texts of the readings), (Oxford, 1983)

PHILIP, N. and NEUBERG, V. (eds.) *A December Vision: And Other Thoughtful Writings* (Continuum, 1987)

THOMAS, D. (ed.) *Selected Short Fiction* (Penguin Classics, 1976)

Biography and criticism

BUTT, J. and TILLOTSON, K. *Dickens at Work* (Methuen, 1985)

GRANT, A. *A Preface to Dickens* (Longman, 1986)

JOHNSON, E. *Charles Dickens: His Tragedy and Triumph* (Penguin, 1986)

KAPLAN, F. *Dickens, A Biography* (Morrow, 1988)

LEAVIS, F.R. and Q.D. *Dickens the Novelist* (Rutgers Univ. Press, 1979)

MACKENZIE N. and J. *Dickens: A Life* (Oxford, 1979)

ORWELL, G. "Charles Dickens" (Penguin, 1965)

PAROISSIEN, D. (ed.) *Selected Letters of Charles Dickens* (Tudyne, 1985)

PRIESTLEY, J.B. *Charles Dickens and His World* (Thames & Hudson, 1978)

SLATER, M. *Dickens and Women* (Stanford Univ. Press, 1983)

WILSON, A. *The World of Charles Dickens* (Penguin, 1972)

Further Information

Films and Videos

Dickens's novels have often been made into films. Several film versions exist for some titles, including: *A Tale of Two Cities, Oliver Twist, Pickwick Papers, Great Expectations* and *A Christmas Carol*. Many of these films are currently available on video.

Museums in England

The Dickens House Museum, 48 Doughty Street, London WC1N 2LF. This is the center for Dickens studies, where Dickens wrote *Oliver Twist* and *Nicholas Nickleby*, and where Mary Hogarth died.
The Charles Dickens Centre, High Street, Rochester, Kent. A Dickens Festival is held in Rochester every June.
There are other Dickens Museums in Portsmouth (his birthplace) and in Broadstairs, Kent.

Index

Picture acknowledgments

The author and publishers would like to thank the following for allowing their illustrations to be reproduced in this book: The Dickens House Museum 7, 8, 13, 15, 16, 18, 20, 21, 22, 23, 25, 26, 28, 30, 32, 34, 37, 39, 41, 43, 44, 45, 46, 47, 49, 52, 53, 54, 58, 65, 68, 71, 75, 78, 79, 80, 82, 84, 85, 86, 92, 94, 96, 97, 98, 99; The Mansell Historical Collection 10, 72, 73, 91; Mary Evans Picture Library 51, 67; The National Film Archive 36, 56, 62, 76, 87, 89; The Victoria and Albert Museum 35, 61; Wayland Picture Library 12, 59, 60.

First published in the
United States in 1990 by
The Rourke Corporation, Inc.
Vero Beach, FL 32964

Printed in Italy by G. Canale & C.S.p.A. Turin